Karsten Tischer

Setting in Charles Dickens' "Hard Times"

GRIN Verlag

Bibliografische Information der Deutschen Nationalbibliothek:

Die Deutsche Bibliothek verzeichnet diese Publikation in der Deutschen National-
bibliografie; detaillierte bibliografische Daten sind im Internet über http://dnb.d-
nb.de/ abrufbar.

Imprint:

Copyright © 2007 GRIN Verlag GmbH
Druck und Bindung: Books on Demand GmbH, Norderstedt Germany
ISBN: 978-3-640-45198-2

This book at GRIN:

http://www.grin.com/en/e-book/110923/setting-in-charles-dickens-hard-times

Winter Semester 2006/07

The Social Novel in 19th Century England

Setting in Charles Dickens' *Hard Times.*

Karsten Tischer

Subjects: German, English
(6th semester)

Date of Submission:
15 June 2007

Table of Contents

Evidences of citations from the primary text are made directly behind the relevant phrase(s) in brackets. For all citations from secondary literature footnotes are used.

For the sake of fluent reading in cases when both genders are meant, only the masculine forms of the particular pronouns are used. That means, for instance, "his" instead of "his/her".

1. Introduction

Charles Dickens was born on the 7th of February 1812 and the British Empire was about to become the greatest empire on the planet.[1] Unfortunately not all citizens have profited from this development. Dickens himself had to quit school and started his work in *Warren's Blacking Factory*, a period in his life which had – by his own comments – a huge impact on his lifetime and on his works thus, too.[2] His biographer and friend John Forster also points out this factor.[3] This assumption correlates with the sociology of the Frenchman Hippolyte Taine (1828 – 1893) who has said that each individual is determined by the three factors: *race, milieu* and *moment.* Stronger related to literary criticism Wilhelm Scherer (1841 –1886) had searched explicitly in the lives of authors for reasons which explain their works.[4]

Especially *Hard Times* which was written in 1854 is strongly suitable because it mirrors these bad experiences Dickens made during his life.[5] It reflects firstly the current conflict between the class of the working people (*proletariat*) and the smaller class of the manufacturers (*bourgeoisie*), secondly the sympathy for the first group resulting from his own youth. In a letter to Charles Knight (17th March 1854) he wrote: "The English are, so far as I know, the hardest worked people on whom the sun shines. [...] They are born at the oar, and they live and die at it."[6] Hans Ulrich Seeber adds that English society decayed into two parts which know almost nothing about each other.[7] Dickens wanted to give a signal which should wake up both sides to stop this development before a revolution would destroy much more.[8]

To guarantee an impact on his readers it seems obvious that he has to describe the *milieu* and the *moment* of the story in a prominent way. Thus, especially the setting of *Hard Times* is worth to take a closer look at.

---

[1] Franz Lenze, "Mutter des Imperiums," *GEO EPOCHE* 18 (2005): 140.

[2] Annegret Maack, *Charles Dickens, Epoche-Werk-Wirkung* (München: Beck, 1991) 37.

[3] Maack 38.

[4] B. Jeßing, et al. *Einführung in die Neuere deutsche Literaturwissenschaft.* 2nd ed. (Stuttgart: Metzler, 2007) 74.

[5] Maack 38.

[6] G. Storey, et al. *The Letters of Charles Dickens, Vol. 7 (1853-1855)* (Oxford: Clarendon Press, 1993) 294.

[7] Hans Ulrich Seeber, "Der Sozialroman," *Englische Literaturgeschichte,* ed. Hans Ulrich Seeber. 4th ed. (Stuttgart: Metzler, 2004) 277.

[8] Maack 126, 128.

Besides the economic discrepancy between the two classes Dickens adds the contrast between the world of the people who see only *facts* as the only reality and the world of the group of people who hold up another than the real world – the realm of *fancy*.

With the aim to characterize and separate the antagonists from each other Dickens uses among other things the *setting* which offers him the opportunity to do so in an indirect way. This transfers the task of interpreting the *hard times* and their causes to the reader's mind.

2. Setting in Narrative Texts

In most books which are concerned with the analysis of narrative texts the field of *setting* is often one which finds only little attention. "[F]or a long time, the general assumption was that a verbal narrative's setting simply is not as important as its temporal framework and chronology."[9]

This belief is outdated. Not at last social/industrial novels like *Hard Times* or *Mary Barton* by Elizabeth Gaskell could only function with the background of the time they were written in.

This importance of *setting* can easily underlined by the determinants introduced by Hippolyte Taine. In relation to setting especially *milieu* and *moment* are decisive. Hence the environment of an individual has got active influence on his imprinting – it is forming his character.

M. H. Abrams distinguishes *setting* into "the general locale, historical time, and social circumstances in which its action occurs"[10] and "the setting of a single episode or scene"[11]. This sounds rather abstract but it covers a huge variety of different aspects. Every little detail, such as weather, houses, a whole town and its countryside or the interior of a single room can tell the reader something important about the person who lives there.[12] Besides the simple arrangement of, for instance, a room, it is also of great importance how the narrator presents it. An apartment by night looks different than at noon. Hence it definitely depends on the narrator how he presents it. "Setting can reveal the author's view of the world [...]"[13], as Richard Gill explains. This is exactly the case when we look at *Hard Times*. For an author like Dickens it was of extreme importance to convey a critical view on the time he was living in.[14]

---

[9] Manfred Jahn, 2005, *Narratology, A Guide to the Theory of Narrative,* English Department, University of Cologne, <http://www.uni-koeln.de/~ame02/pppn.htm>.

[10] M. H. Abrams, *A Glossary of Literary Terms,* 7th ed. (Orlando: Harcourt Brace College Publishers, 1998) 284.

[11] Abrams 284.

[12] Richard Gill, *Mastering English Literature* (London: Macmillian, 1990) 106.

[13] Gill 111.

[14] Maack 126.

He "uses setting to show how a character is situated"[15]. Gerhard Hoffmann speaks of *gestimmter Raum* as a symbol of analogy between space and character.[16] Here the room/space has got a symbolic meaning which can contrast it with another place.[17] Moreover place is "*Aktionsraum*"[18] where the action which "must have a specific locale to occur in"[19] happens and of course, a character needs a place to live in. It forms among other things his identity[20] as a "'lived space' or *erlebter Raum*"[21]. Finally the setting "is established by fixed descriptions or by indirect references in the narrative or in the speeches of characters"[22].

---

[15] Gill 109.

[16] Winfried Spiegel, *Der Raum des Fortschritts und der Unnatur, Die Industriestadt im viktorianischen Roman* (Trier: Wissenschaftlicher Verlag, 1992) 136.

[17] Birgit Haupt, "Zur Analyse des Raums," *Einführung in die Erzähltextanalyse, Kategorien, Modelle, Probleme,* ed. Peter Wenzel. (Trier: Wissenschaftlicher Verlag, 2004) 85.

[18] Haupt 72.

[19] Leonard Lutwack, *The Role of Place in Literature,* (New York: Syracuse University Press, 1984) 17.

[20] Lutwack 17.

[21] Lutwack 27.

[22] Lutwack 74.

3. The World of *Facts*

3.1 Hard Times for These Times

As the full title of Charles Dickens' novel reveals, even for the difficult times the people were living in, the middle of the 19th century was harder than progress would have justified. Even though the industrial production in Great Britain increased from £230,000,000 (1800) to £577,000,000 (1860) not only the working people (*proletariat*) had the impression that solely a small group (*bourgeoisie*) profited by this rapid change.[23] The class society became the new social system.[24] George Bernard Shaw formulates it less abstractly: "Here you will find [...] only oppressors and victims [...]"[25] living side by side in "the wickedest of all the centuries"[26].

To get a picture of the daily routine of an English worker, the report *Die Lage der arbeitenden Klasse in England* by Friedrich Engels is very helpful. Although he had visited Manchester and not Preston – the city which was the inspiration for Coketown where the story of *Hard Times* takes place – his report is yet worth mentioning. On the one hand Preston is located only about 40 kilometres away from the industrial city of Manchester and on the other hand Engels had written down his impressions in 1844/45 – thus only ten years before Dickens worked up his.[27]

The cities grew as a result of industrialisation and already before by the huge increase of the European population since the 18th century.[28] The city was the place where work was to be found. Promoted by the end of the domestic system in the cotton manufacture around Manchester, which led to a wide spread industry, a centralisation of the production was guaranteed and thus, urbanisation was made possible in this region.[29] And of course, the invention of the steam engine was another prerequisite for a concentration in one place.[30]

A simple comparison reflects how fast this development happened: In 1786 there was only one chimney of a factory to see in Manchester; in 1801 there were 50.[31] Unfortunately the

---

[23] K. D. Hein-Mooren, et al. *Von der Französischen Revolution bis zum Nationalsozialismus* (Bamberg: C.C. Buchners Verlag, 1996) 163.

[24] Hein-Mooren 170.

[25] G. Ford, et al. *Hard Times* (New York: Norton, 1966) 334.

[26] Ford 332.

[27] F. Engels, et al. *Werke*, Bd. 2 (Berlin/DDR: Dietz, 1972) 278.

[28] Hein-Mooren 144.

[29] Spiegel 18.

[30] Hein-Mooren 155.

[31] Hein-Mooren 163.

growth of the industry was too fast for most cities. They all had the problem to construct new and secure houses for the masses of workers. The result was that the ugliest buildings were created in claustrophobic narrowness. Engels describes them as dirty and almost completely ruined[32] and Richard D. Altick speaks of an "imprisonment in the slums"[33]. Regrettably this is no exaggeration. In the middle of the 19th century more English people live in cities than in the country for the first time ever.[34] The working people spent at least six days a week in the factory and not seldom more than fifteen hours per day[35] for a wage which was almost completely used up to buy food[36] which was that what the bourgeoisie decided to be of too bad quality for themselves.[37]

Therefore Dickens uses this novel and more precisely the "Explorationsperspektive"[38] to introduce the higher classes to the workers' world to establish an understanding of each other.[39] This point of view was, of course justified by the inhuman conditions mentioned above, a rather dark one, which has its origin in the expeditions during the colonial age which have lightened up dark unknown regions, especially on the continent of Africa.[40]

The image of the city has totally changed with the industrial revolution. "Originally designed as a haven of security for community […] the city has become […] a demonic monstrosity."[41] "Instead of finding community […] the individual finds indifference, isolation, and confinement."[42] "Man, once creator, becomes the object, while man's created object, the city, becomes the active subject of these works."[43] "Nature is set *against* culture."[44]

---

[32] Engels 280.

[33] Richard D. Altick, *Victorian People and Ideas* (London: Dent & Son, 1974) 40.

[34] Spiegel 19.

[35] Hein-Mooren 171.

[36] Engels 304.

[37] Engels 299.

[38] Uwe Böker, "Von Wordsworths schlummerndem London bis zum Abgrund der Jahrhundertwende, Die Stadt in der englischen Literatur des 19. Jahrhunderts," *Die Stadt in der Literatur,* eds. Cord Meckseper and Elisabeth Schraut. (Göttingen: Vandenhoeck & Ruprecht, 1983) 32.

[39] Seeber 277.

[40] Böker 38.

[41] "City," *Themes & Motifs in Western Literature, A Handbook,* 1987 ed.

[42] "City".

[43] "City".

[44] Gerhard Hoffmann, "Space as Form and Force in the Novel," *Space-Place-Environment,* eds. Lothar Hönnighausen, Julia Apitzsch and Wibke Reger. (Tübingen: Stauffenburg Verlag, 2004) 147.

3.2 Coketown – A Triumph of Fact

Coketown is the "general locale"[45] of Dickens' novel but even though it is fictional, it shows strong relations to reality. The majority of the experts represent the opinion that the creation of Coketown was inspired by the city of Preston. Dickens was attracted by a "strike which had broken out in the industrial north of England"[46]. He visited "Preston, a textile-manufacturing town in Lancashire [...]"[47] and wrote about his experiences in a letter to John Forster (29th January 1854):

> Except the crowds at the street-corners reading the placards pro and con; and the cold absence of smoke from the mill-chimneys; there is very little in the streets to make the town remarkable. [...] [T]he people 'sit at home and mope.' [...] I shall return. It is a nasty place (I thought it was a model town) [...].[48]

This quotation proves on the one hand that Dickens was there when he worked on *Hard Times* but on the other hand he sounds rather disappointed about the town and its inhabitants. Additionally Dickens finds himself misunderstood when people say that Coketown refers to Preston. In a letter to Peter Cunningham (11th March 1854) Dickens makes clear that "[...] chapters of the story were written, before I went to Preston or thought about the present strike."[49] He also warns about the "mischief of such a statement [...]"[50] because "it localizes [...] a story which has a direct purpose in reference to the working people all over England, and it will cause, as I know by former experience, characters to be fitted on to individuals whom I never saw or heard of in my life."[51] Of course he was right, the first page of *Hard Times* was written on the 23rd of January – six days before his visit[52] but the Preston strike already began in 1853 and in another letter Dickens wrote to Miss Coutts at the end of November 1853 about the "obnoxious manufacturers of Preston"[53]. Thus it seems obvious that he already heard something about the strike before his visit but perhaps found some inspiration for *his* town from other industrial towns of this type.

---

[45] Abrams 284.

[46] Ford 278.

[47] Ford 278.

[48] Storey 260f.

[49] Ford 275.

[50] Ford 275.

[51] Ford 275.

[52] Ford 270.

[53] Ford 272.

However, Coketown belongs to the fictional world of the novel and it can be only seen as a device to characterize the time and the characters. It is a *gestimmter Raum* where every little element seems to have a deeper meaning which should activate the reader's attention. But at the first time the narrator advances to the "demonic"[54] maze very carefully. From his "panoramic view"[55], as Manfred Jahn calls it, the authorial narrator describes Coketown from the distance: "It was a town of red brick, or of brick that would have been red if the smoke and ashes had allowed it; but as matters stood it was a town of unnatural red and black like the painted face of a savage" (Dickens, 28). This means firstly that the narrator does not belong to this world because the general attitude of the men of letters was very "anti-urban"[56] and secondly Coketown substantiates the common image of an industrial town of this period. Many Victorian authors were heavily influenced by Romanticism where the industrial town was seen as purely unnatural.[57]

Smoke and *ashes* disturb the sight of the human beings and of course, pollute not only nature but the lungs of the workers as well. The *smoke* and the *ashes* cover the buildings which were formerly red but now rather black. Formulating it more precisely, the smoke and the ashes in Coketown come mostly from the chimneys of the factories which form the townscape. James Lowe wrote that there were about "fifty tall chimneys"[58] in Preston at the time of the lock-out.

This must have been a real unnatural picture but why has Dickens chosen the simile of the "painted face of a savage" (Dickens, 28) for his description? This phrase contains – like others, for instance, "serpents of smoke" (Dickens, 28) which are ejected by the "tall chimneys" (Dickens, 28) and the "elephant" (Dickens, 28) whose movements are compared with the "monotonous[…] up and down" (Dickens, 28) of the steam-engines in the manufactory – items of the jungle. A human civilisation gave way to the law of the stronger that *only the fittest survive*. The "decay is expressed by metaphors of fire, furnace, and ash."[59] If this is still an urban jungle or already *hell on earth* is discussible. In a jungle anybody fights for his own survival. People get reduced to their primeval instincts and lose their identity.[60] A town where dirt is everywhere, where the work "murder[s] the innocents" (Dickens, 3), can certainly not become something as *homeland* to the citizens to identify with. Therefore Coketown is more

---

[54] "City".

[55] Jahn, *Narratology*.

[56] Spiegel 124.

[57] Spiegel 124.

[58] Ford 284.

[59] "City".

[60] Till R. Kuhnle, "Ekelhafte Stadtansichten," *Die andere Stadt, Großstadtbilder in der Perspektive des peripheren Blicks,* eds. Albrecht Buschmann and Dieter Ingenschay. (Würzburg: Königshausen & Neumann GmbH, 2000) 144.

like a *modern hell* where the Hands work in the "hot mill[s]" (Dickens, 92). John Milton describes in 'Paradise Lost' the hell as a place where darkness dominates and only gleaming flames give light in a threatening way. Down there Satan lords it over serpents.[61] This description from 1667 seems more present than ever before. There are other hellish things like the "black canal [...] with ill-smelling dye" (Dickens, 28). It is a *canal* which was probably a *river* some day until human beings straightened it. The "monstrous serpents of smoke" (Dickens, 91) around the chimneys "never [...] uncoiled" (Dickens, 28). The chimneys themselves are "rising up into the air like competing Towers of Babel" (Dickens, 107). Nevertheless it is not easy to have a look at these monsters. Coketown lies in "a haze of its own" (Dickens, 146) impossible to penetrate for the sun rays. Thus, they cannot spend the essential light to grow anything natural. The town was only a "mass[...] of darkness" (Dickens, 146) and therefore cannot be seen from the distance.

Hence the narrator starts his expedition and explores the city in detail. He sees everywhere the *same* things: "pavements" (Dickens, 28), "streets all very like one another" (Dickens, 28) and "people equally like one another" (Dickens, 28). Everything looks the *same*. The external monotony of the city of Coketown corresponds to the internal monotony of the working people.[62] These are perfect examples where rooms/spaces function as analogies to the characters who live in them.[63] A dull town architecture was very common for the time. It guarantees a uniform and replaceable appearance of the particular town.[64] Like the structure of the town let's suppose, horizontal places in general are seen as rather "uninspiring"[65] and boring.

3.3 Bounderby – A Man of Coketown

Despite his own appellation as *Josiah Bounderby of Coketown* he is in fact as a mill-owner a striking part of the city but in truth he lives "about fifteen miles from the town" (Dickens, 222). Hence out of the reach of the "serpents of smoke" (Dickens, 28) which pollute the air.

Leonard Lutwack speaks of "[a]-centrality"[66] which is the "opposite of the central place"[67]; here: Coketown. "The peripheral place may be a refuge"[68] to flee from the "workaday world"[69]

---

[61] Herbert Vorgrimler, *Geschichte der Hölle* (München: Fink, 1993) 371.

[62] Spiegel 137.

[63] Spiegel 136.

[64] Spiegel 22.

[65] Lutwack 41.

[66] Lutwack 44.

where Bounderby lets others work, either in the factories or in his bank ("another red brick house" [Dickens, 149]) where the profits are managed.

His "private red brick dwelling" (Dickens, 168) has "the black outside shutters, the green inside blinds, and the black street door up the two white steps" (Dickens, 168). It fits perfectly into the monotony of Coketown and looks almost the same like his bank. The black shutters and the black street door are rather uninviting. Bounderby apparently wants to keep away any strangers who want to have a look inside or even steal something. The white steps appear innocent and clean as the *red* of the walls but only because the dust and the ashes from the chimneys have never reached them.

Inside the "red brick castle of the giant Bounderby" (Dickens, 192) hang "pictures with his origin […] among the elegant furniture" (Dickens, 223). There he and Mrs. Sparsit live their illusions of great careers. The one who says he came directly from a "ditch" (Dickens, 19) and the other who serves the first named as a noble Powler.

The contradictions proceed with the "stabling […] for a dozen horses" (Dickens, 223) and a "flower-garden" (Dickens, 223) where they "grow cabbages" (Dickens, 223). This is mere scorn for the workers but of course, fulfils the image the narrator wants to convey.

---

[67] Lutwack 44.

[68] Lutwack 45.

[69] Lutwack 45.

4. Between *Heaven* and *Hell*

A metaphor the narrator uses very frequently in *Hard Times* is that of going *up* or *down* stairs which corresponds with the fate of a character. This image is a very traditional one. Even "in the Old Testament angels descend from heaven on a stairway"[70]. The top stands for *heaven* (the good) and the bottom for *hell* (the bad).[71] Both places "are absolutely opposed while earth has qualities of both"[72] and can therefore be inhabited by both the circus and Coketown.

There are many examples in the text but the basic principle will be illustrated only with the most important one: Mrs. Sparsit's *staircase*.

It seems ridiculous that someone like Mrs. Sparsit creates a staircase with her fancy "to watch Louisa coming down" (Dickens, 269) "to the black gulf at the bottom" (Dickens, 274) which will wash her away from the side of Mr. Bounderby. So Mrs. Sparsit spies on Jem and Loo and she runs like never (!) before and finds both in the wood. "The forest lying beyond the garden is another place of great sexual significance."[73] It "signifies an unruly sexuality that threatens tragedy for those who become involved with it."[74]

Unfortunately rain and an upcoming thunderstorm disturb the observation. Mrs. Sparsit has to hurry again to follow "Miss Gradgrind" (Dickens, 249). Loo enters the train which comes with "[f]ire and steam, and smoke, and *red* light" (Dickens, 284) and finally finds her final destination in the arms of Thomas Gradgrind, her father who was more often in London, the capital of the world, than at the deathbed of his wife.[75] Eventually Louisa falls with a "wild dilating fire in the eyes" (Dickens, 291) and a roaring thunderstorm outside "on the floor" (Dickens, 292) but without Mrs. Sparsit as a snoopy witness. She lost her trace on the streets which were "under water" (Dickens, 285). Everything was washed away as if a "deluge" (Dickens, 286) cleaned Coketown.

---

[70] Lutwack 103.

[71] Lutwack 39.

[72] Lutwack 39.

[73] Lutwack 99.

[74] Lutwack 99.

[75] Lenze 148.

5. The World of Fancy - The Circus, A Circle in a Square City

The word *circus* is derived from the Latin word *circus* which means *ring* or *circle*.[76] Hence its bare shape forms a contradiction to the city of Coketown. *Sleary's Horse-riding* just makes a stop in the town. It is situated on "neutral ground [...] which was neither town nor country" (Dickens, 13). So it does neither really belong to the monotonous industrial city nor to the natural countryside. This fact attests also Sissy Jupe: "We travelled about the country, and had no fixed place to live in" (Dickens, 77).

In former times "circular movements are frequently thought to replicate the circular motion of heavenly bodies"[77] and "circular shapes and motions are frequently assigned a sacred or religious function"[78]. Furthermore the circle is a symbol for divine love, a feeling which a Gradgrind could only hardly imagine.[79] The narrator takes this religious tradition on and uses it as a contrast to the Gradgrindian world which accepts neither religion nor any religious symbols like angels who fly around in heaven. But just these circus artists earn their money with magic which is beyond the factual, explainable world of *facts*. They balance on the trapeze above the ground and fly through the air; they perform feats with exotic animals and thus differ a lot from the city of Coketown where the people do not live so close to heaven and where nature has become extinct since decades. The children of Thomas Gradgrind do not belong to this world but try to "peep in at the hidden glories of the place" (Dickens, 15). Unfortunately their father catches them in the very act. Consequently Loo and Thomas remain with the burned-in image of a horse which they have learnt in school: an animal with "[f]orty teeth, [...] four eye-teeth, [...] twelve incisive [...] and much more" (Dickens, 6). It is a quadruped which can neither "walk[...] up and down the sides of rooms" (Dickens, 7) nor fly like the mythological *Pegasus* which is a constituent of the name of the public-house, called "the Pegasus's Arms" (Dickens, 36), where the artists live in. In it "dim *red* lights" (Dickens, 35) are glowing which are identifiable as *red* lights even though it was dim; thus, totally different from the red bricks of Coketown which are covered with dust and ashes.

Additionally to the steed outside they have another Pegasus hanging on the wall. It is pictured with wings which are flying through "real gauze" (Dickens, 36) and an "ethereal harness made of red silk" (Dickens, 36). This winged horse is, of course, far beyond the factual image of a Gradgrindian horse but in addition to the contrast of *fact* and *fancy* it tells the reader

---

[76] "circus," *Stowasser, 2004* ed.

[77] "Circle," *Encyclopedia of Religion*, 2nd ed. 2005.

[78] „Circle".

[79] "Kreis," *Lexikon der christlichen Ikonographie,* 1994 ed.

which of the two is the better image because Pegasus wears a "harness made of *red* silk" (Dickens, 36) whereas the buildings of Coketown were formerly also *red* but now there is no *red* visible anymore.

The mythological *Pegasus* was a winged steed. Its father was *Poseidon*, god of the sea. For many Greeks he was also god of the horses and they even said that he has created the horse.[80] This could be an allusion of the narrator that the circus possesses the better version of a horse even though it is not realistic. The mother of *Pegasus* was *Medusa*, an ogre which had serpents as hair. Everybody who looked it in the eyes was transfixed immediately.[81] Now the comparison to Coketown seems attractive. The town, where masses of houses made of stone eliminate nature and where "serpents of smoke" (Dickens, 28) are blown out of the "tall chimneys" (Dickens, 28) every day, appears as an allusion to the mythological monster. Finally the most adequate myth about the winged steed which forms a parallel to the life in Coketown is probably the fight against the Chimaera. The Chimaera was an ugly monster as well. It had the head of a lion and the tail of a serpent. Additionally it breathed fire. One day king's son Bellerophon slew the ogre riding on the back of Pegasus.[82] This myth can obviously be transferred into the story. The king's daughter Louisa (with respect for Dickens' accentuation of the importance of women and their "feminine traits"[83], for instance, the love they give) bursts out of the chains her father had tied around her with the help of circus member Cecilia Jupe. Together they fight against the Chimaera whose lion head symbolizes England because it refers to the three lions of the Royal Coat of Arms of the United Kingdom.[84] The fire spitting is certainly an allusion to the smoke which comes out of the chimneys of the factories. Of course, Thomas Gradgrind is not the king of England but he definitely benefits from the current conditions. Secondly Louisa and Sissy do not stop the exploitation of the poor Hands but they demolish the philosophy of Loo's father, anyhow.

Nevertheless Pegasus keeps an offspring of *Medusa*, or to transfer it to *Hard Times*, the circus was once a part of Coketown but has developed in a completely different direction. It reflects rather the positive features of human life. When Sissy recognizes that her father is gone, Sleary provides her immediately after Thomas Gradgrind's plan to educate her a counter offer: "Emma Gordon [...] would be a mother to you, and Joth'phine would be a thither to you" (Dickens, 50). They form one big family which stays always together. Everybody is there for

---

[80] Jens Köhn, *Götter, Helden, Ungeheuer*, 2nd ed. (Berlin: Kinderbuchverlag, 1990) 67f.

[81] Köhn 50.

[82] Köhn 24.

[83] SparkNotes, *Hard Times, Charles Dickens, Themes, Motifs & Symbols* <http://www.sparknotes.com/lit/hardtimes/themes.html>.

[84] Wikipedia, The Free Encyclopedia, *Royal coat of arms of the United Kingdom* <http://en.wikipedia.org/wiki/Royal_Coat_of_Arms_of_the_United_Kingdom>.

each other and cares about each member of the group. Thus it is totally different to the isolated world of Coketown. Additionally the narrator enforces this discrepancy when he enumerates the "members of Sleary's *company*" (Dickens, 45): "two or three husbands, and their two or three mothers, and their eight or nine little children" (Dickens, 45) appear "from the upper regions" (Dickens, 45). This vagueness expressed by the 'or' stands in total contradiction to the demand of accuracy of the Gradgrindian philosophy. Furthermore, the circumstance that the circus people have to come down from their "upper regions" (Dickens, 45) to listen to Bounderby and Gradgrind virtually flouts the gap between the two classes.

Dickens enlarged the difference between both by using a slightly different language for the circus members. On the 20th of February 1854 Dickens wrote a letter to Mark Lemon including the request to send him "any slang terms among tumblers and Circus-people"[85]. "I have noted down some–I want them in my new story"[86]. The verbal disadvantage of the circus people is most clearly apparent when Sleary speaks. He "was troubled with asthma, and whose breath came far too thick and heavy for the letter s" (Dickens, 46). Nevertheless his mistake makes him more likeable than it disturbs.

Even if the circus appears only at the beginning and at the end of the novel, Sissy represents this place like a personification of it through the whole story.[87] Thus, the circus is the strongest opponent of the factual world. It stands for imagination, the quality which makes up the major difference between human beings and lower animals.[88] With this imagination the circus hides "the often shabby reality behind the fanciful show"[89] and is therefore an active contribution to the revival of the exploited people, for instance, young Thomas Gradgrind who can escape with the circus's help.

---

[85] Storey 279.

[86] Storey 279.

[87] Maack 143.

[88] Maack 144.

[89] Catherine Gallagher, *The Industrial Revolution of English Fiction, 1832-1867,* (Chicago: The University of Chicago Press, 1988) 162.

6. Conclusion

"I believe […] that into the relations between employers and employed, as into all the relations of this life, there must enter something of feeling and sentiment […]."[90] These were Dickens' words to a man he met in the train going down to Preston and he truly contributes something to this statement with his novel *Hard Times*. He alludes to the inhuman conditions of the Hands and stands for a change in educating the people who will be the future of the whole country. To make this obvious he operates with the contrast between fact and fancy and lets his narrator take a firm stand on the side of the poor. And he does that with a certain irony. While Bounderby and the town of Coketown pretend to be something different than they really are, the circus is the only true reality.[91]

Unfortunately it was impossible to cover all uses of places in the novel. There are many more but the major aspect was upon the two opponents – Coketown and the circus. To find a conclusion anyhow, it should be said that Dickens created many places which were almost never only background for the actions, they were *gestimmte Räume* which determined each character. There was always an interaction between both and thus, Taine's theory finds confirmation in this novel.

---

[90] Ford 288.
[91] Maack 149.

7. Bibliography

Primary literature

Dickens, Charles. *Hard Times.* Oxford: Oxford University Press, 1998.

Secondary literature

Abrams, M. H. *A Glossary of Literary Terms.* 7th ed. Orlando: Harcourt Brace College Publishers, 1998.

Altick, Richard D. *Victorian People and Ideas.* London: Dent & Son, 1974.

Böker, Uwe. "Von Wordsworths schlummerndem London bis zum Abgrund der Jahrhundertwende. Die Stadt in der englischen Literatur des 19. Jahrhunderts." *Die Stadt in der Literatur.* Eds. Cord Meckseper and Elisabeth Schraut. Göttingen: Vandenhoeck & Ruprecht, 1983. 28-56.

"Circle." *Encyclopedia of Religion.* 2nd ed. 2005.

"circus." *Stowasser. Lateinisch – deutsches Schulwörterbuch.* 2004 ed.

"City." *Themes & Motifs in Western Literature. A Handbook.* 1987 ed.

Dickens, Charles. *Hard Times.* Ed. George Ford and Sylvère Monod. New York: Norton, 1966.

Gallagher, Catherine. *The Industrial Reformation of English Fiction. 1832-1867.* Chicago: The University of Chicago Press, 1988.

Gill, Richard. *Mastering English Literature.* London: Macmillian, 1990.

Haupt, Birgit. "Zur Analyse des Raums." *Einführung in die Erzähltextanalyse. Kategorien, Modelle, Probleme.* Ed. Peter Wenzel. Trier: Wissenschaftlicher Verlag, 2004. 69-87.

Hein-Mooren, K. D., et al. *Von der Französischen Revolution bis zum Nationalsozialismus.* Bamberg: C.C. Buchners, 1996.

Hoffmann, Gerhard. "Space as Form and Force in the Novel." *Space-Place-Environment.* Eds. Lothar Hönnighausen, Julia Apitzsch and Wibke Reger. Tübingen: Stauffenburg Verlag, 2004. 137-156.

Jahn, Manfred. 2005. Narratology: A Guide to the Theory of Narrative. English Department, University of Cologne. <http://www.uni-koeln.de/~ame02/pppn.htm> (22 Mar 2007).

Jeßing, B., et al. *Einführung in die Neuere deutsche Literaturwissenschaft.* 2nd ed. Stuttgart: Metzler, 2007.

Köhn, Jens. *Götter, Helden, Ungeheuer.* 2nd ed. Berlin: Kinderbuchverlag, 1990.

"Kreis." *Lexikon der christlichen Ikonographie.* 1994 ed.

Kuhnle, Till R. "Ekelhafte Stadtansichten." *Die andere Stadt. Großstadtbilder in der Perspektive des peripheren Blicks.* Eds. Albrecht Buschmann and Dieter Ingenschay. Würzburg: Königshausen & Neumann GmbH, 2000. 144-156.
Lenze, Franz. "Mutter des Imperiums." *GEO EPOCHE* 18 (2005): 140-153.

Lutwack, Leonard. *The Role of Place in Literature.* New York: Syracuse University Press, 1984.

Maack, Annegret. *Charles Dickens. Epoche – Werk – Wirkung.* München: Beck, 1991.

Marx, K. and F. Engels. *Werke.* Bd. 2. Berlin/DDR: Dietz, 1972.

Seeber, Hans Ulrich. "Der Sozialroman." *Englische Literaturgeschichte.* Ed. Hans Ulrich Seeber. 4th ed. Stuttgart: Metzler, 2004. 277-280.

SparkNotes. "Hard Times, Charles Dickens, Themes, Motifs & Symbols." <http://www.sparknotes.com/lit/hardtimes/themes.html> (15th June 2007).

Spiegel, Winfried. *Der Raum des Fortschritts und der Unnatur. Die Industriestadt im viktorianischen Roman.* Trier: Wissenschaftlicher Verlag, 1992.

Storey, G., K. Tillotson and A. Easson, eds. *The Letters of Charles Dickens. Vol. 7 (1853-1855).* Oxford: Clarendon Press, 1993.

Vorgrimler, Herbert. *Geschichte der Hölle.* München: Fink, 1993.

Wikipedia. The Free Encyclopedia. "Royal coat of arms of the United Kingdom." <http://en.wikipedia.org/wiki/Royal_Coat_of_Arms_of_the_United_Kingdom> (15th June 2007).